MY VERY OWN ROSH HASHANAH BOOK
by
Judyth Robbins Saypol
Madeline Wikler

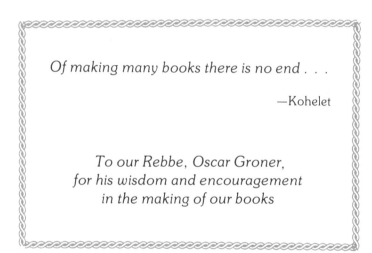

Of making many books there is no end . . .

—Kohelet

*To our Rebbe, Oscar Groner,
for his wisdom and encouragement
in the making of our books*

KAR-BEN COPIES, INC.   ROCKVILLE, MD

Library of Congress Cataloging in Publication Data

Saypol, Judyth R.
  My very own Rosh Hashanah book.

  Summary: Explains the significance of Rosh Hashanah, a ten-day period celebrating the coming of the new year. Includes stories, songs, prayers, and a home service.
    1. Rosh ha-Shanah—Juvenile literature. [1. Rosh ha-Shanah. 2. Judaism—Customs and practices. 3. Fasts and feasts—Judaism] I. Wikler, Madeline, 1943-
II. Title.
BM695.N5S28 1983   296.4'31   83-26748
ISBN 0-930494-06-7 (pbk.)

Rosh Hashanah and Yom Kippur are not children's holidays. The ideas they express are difficult even for adults. Yet children are aware that these are the central religious holidays of the Jewish year. They stay home from school. They participate in family celebrations and the sending and receiving of *Shanah Tovah* cards. They attend children's synagogue services.

Our books — one for each of the holidays — should be seen as resources to help young children understand such Rosh Hashanah and Yom Kippur ideas as renewal, forgiveness, repentence, responsibility. Both the narrative and the *Chassidic* stories which illustrate many of the High Holy Day themes can be used as starting points for family or classroom discussion.

J.R.S.
M.W.

**E**veryone loves to celebrate birthdays. Rosh Hashanah is a special birthday. It is the birthday of the world.

When does the year begin?

The Jewish year has many beginnings.

Nisan, the month when *Pesach* is celebrated is the first month of the Jewish calendar. It is the beginning of spring.

Animals celebrate their birthdays on the first of *Elul.*

Trees celebrate on the holiday of *Tu B'Shevat.*

Tishri begins the new year for people and for the counting of years. This new year is called Rosh Hashanah.

The *Torah* tells us—

> *On the first day of the seventh month (Tishri) you shall not do any work. You shall celebrate and sound the Shofar.*

Rosh Hashanah comes in the fall, usually in September, but sometimes as late as October. It begins a ten-day period called the High Holy Days which ends with Yom Kippur. Some people celebrate Rosh Hashanah for two days. Others celebrate for one day.

osh Hashanah is known by many names and descriptions. The name Rosh Hashanah means the "head" or beginning of the year. We say good-bye to the old year and welcome a new year—

A gift of time.

A new opportunity to learn and to grow.

Another name for Rosh Hashanah is *Yom Teruah*—the Day of the Blowing of the *Shofar.* We blow the *Shofar* in the synagogue to welcome the new year.

A third name is *Yom Hazikaron,* the Day of Remembering. Jewish people believe that on this day God thinks about the world He created.

Finally, Rosh Hashanah is known as *Yom Hadin,* the Day of Judgment. God remembers the deeds of all people and judges the world for the coming year.

Rosh Hashanah is a happy time. We welcome the new year in a family celebration.

It is also a serious time. We think about ourselves, what we have done the past year, and how we can do better in the year ahead.

There was once a man who was quite forgetful. When he got up in the morning, he never remembered where he left his clothes.

One night he thought of a plan. He took paper and pencil, and, as he undressed, he wrote down exactly where he put all his clothes.

The next morning he was very pleased. He took the piece of paper and read the list.

"Cap." There it was.

"Pants." He found them.

"Shirt." There it lay.

And so it was until he was fully dressed.

"That's fine," he said.

"But now, where am I myself?" he asked very puzzled.

"Where in the world am I?"

He looked and looked, but could not find himself.

Rosh Hashanah gives us a chance to find ourselves.

PREPARING FOR ROSH HASHANAH

**W**e prepare for Rosh Hashanah—at home and in the synagogue—during the entire month of *Elul.*

Beginning on the first of *Elul,* the *Shofar* is blown every day at the end of the morning synagogue service. On the Saturday night before Rosh Hashanah, the community gathers in the synagogue at midnight for *Selichot* prayers. Many of these are sung to the same tunes used on Rosh Hashanah and Yom Kippur. *Selichot* gets us in the mood for the coming holidays.

Once during Elul, the great Rabbi Levi Yitzchak was standing at his window. A shoemaker passed by and asked him, "Have you anything to mend?"

Immediately, Rabbi Levi Yitzchak began to cry. "Woe is me," he wailed. "Rosh Hashanah, the Day of Judgment, is almost here, and I still have not mended myself."

In the villages of Eastern Europe, where many of our grandparents and great grandparents once lived, the month before Rosh Hashanah was a busy time. The whole community looked forward to the coming days with excitement.

Cantors and choirs practiced their chants for the special synagogue services. Booksellers went from village to village selling prayer books and prayer shawls. People collected *tzedakah*, so the poor would have money to buy the things they needed for the holiday.

It was the custom for the *shamash*, the synagogue messenger, to go from house to house to awaken villagers for early morning *Selichot* prayers. Sometimes he knocked on the doors or windows with a special hammer carved in the shape of a *Shofar*.

The children loved to help. Sometimes they would tie a string to their feet and hang one end of the string out the window. The *shamash* would pull the strings to awaken the youngsters, who would follow him on his rounds.

Every Friday during the month of Elul the Rabbi of Nemirov would vanish. He was nowhere to be seen. Where could the Rabbi be?

In heaven, no doubt, the people thought, asking God to bring peace in the New Year.

Where could the Rabbi be? A villager decided to find out.

One night he sneaked into the Rabbi's home, slid under the Rabbi's bed, and waited. Just before dawn, the Rabbi awakened, got out of bed, and began to dress. He put on work pants, high boots, a big hat, a coat, and a wide belt. He put a rope in his pocket, tucked an ax in his belt, and left the house. The villager followed.

The Rabbi crept in the shadows to woods at the edge of town. He took the ax, chopped down a small tree, and split it into logs. Then he bundled the wood, tied it with the rope, put it on his back, and began walking.

He stopped beside a small broken-down shack and knocked at the window.

"Who is there?" asked the frightened, sick woman inside.

"I, Vassil the peasant," answered the Rabbi, entering the house. "I have wood to sell."

"I am a poor widow. Where will I get the money?" she asked.

"I'll lend it to you," replied the Rabbi.

"How will I pay you back?" asked the woman.

"I will trust you," said the Rabbi.

The Rabbi put the wood into the oven, kindled the fire, and left without a word.

Now whenever anyone reports that the Rabbi has gone to heaven, the villager only adds quietly, "Heaven? If not higher."

When a person helps another who is in trouble, the deed is like a prayer.

HOLIDAY GREETINGS

The Rabbis said that beginning in *Elul*, whenever we write someone a letter, we should add our wishes for a good new year. Today, many people make or buy Rosh Hashanah greeting cards to send to family and friends. These cards—of all sizes, shapes, designs, and greetings—are called *Shanah Tovahs*. *Shanah Tovah* means "good year."

There are Jews in the Soviet Union who are not free to celebrate Rosh Hashanah and the other Jewish holidays. We can remember these families by sending them *Shanah Tovah* cards, also.

ROSH HASHANAH AT HOME

Rosh Hashanah is a joyful celebration at home. Families gather for festive meals. Candles are lit, *kiddush* is recited, and *challah* and apples are dipped in honey for a sweet year.

Wearing new clothes and eating fruits new to the season also remind us of the newness of the year.

The *challah* we eat on Rosh Hashanah is different from the long braided *challah* we eat on *Shabbat*. It is round, reminding us of the cycle of the year. Sometimes there is a braided crown around the *challah*, because we speak of God as a ruler or king. Some people bake *challah* with a ladder or a bird on the top in the hope that our prayers will reach heaven.

ROSH HASHANAH IN THE SYNAGOGUE

For Rosh Hashanah services, the Rabbi and Cantor wear white robes called *kittels*. The *Torah* scrolls, too, are dressed in white covers. White stands for forgiveness. We use a special prayerbook called a *machzor*.

In the Rosh Hashanah prayers, we thank God for all the good things He has done for us in the past year. We ask Him for a happy and peaceful year for ourselves, our families, and for all people.

When the synagogue service is over, we greet each other saying, *L'Shanah Tovah Tikatevu*, "May you be written in the Book of Life for a good new year."

One of the most important prayers describes God judging the world. He writes the judgment in the Book of Life.

It is Rosh Hashanah.
God sits on His throne.
He opens a book containing a list of all the things we have done the past year.
The great Shofar is sounded.
As sheep are counted by the shepherd, one by one, each of our lives comes before God.
He judges us for the coming year and writes our judgment in the Book of Life.

Who shall live and who shall die.
Who shall be rich and who shall be poor.

The Book is kept open for ten days.
We have the power to change the judgment through good deeds and helping others.
At the end of Yom Kippur, the Book is closed.

On Rosh Hashanah when it was time to blow the Shofar, the Great Rabbi Levi Yitzhack stood silent on the bimah. The people waited and waited, and nothing happened. They waited some more and still the Rabbi did not begin.

Finally the Cantor approached the Rabbi and asked him what was causing the delay.

The Rabbi whispered. "A young child just came into the synagogue. He is seated near the door. I overheard him talking. This is what he said:

God of the World—
I do not know how to pray.
I do not know what to say.
I only know the 22 letters of the alphabet.
Let me say them to You.
Aleph, Bet, Gimel, Dalet…

I give You these letters. Please join them together to make up a prayer that will be pleasing to You.

"The child recited the alphabet to the very end," said Rabbi Levi Yitzchak. "God is busy now composing his prayer. We must wait until He is finished. Then we will blow the Shofar."

God accepts all prayers that come from our hearts.

BLOWING THE SHOFAR

The *Shofar* is made from the curved horn of a ram or goat. It is a hard instrument to blow, and takes a lot of practice.

In ancient Israel, the *Shofar* was used to announce the new moon and holidays, to signal armies, and to call people to attention.

We blow the *Shofar* on Rosh Hashanah—

> To announce the beginning of the High Holy Days.
>
> To remind us that God is our ruler and judge.
>
> To warn us that we need to improve.

The blowing of the *Shofar* is very dramatic. The *Baal Tekiyah*, the master of the blowing, faces the Holy Ark. He recites the prayers for the blowing of the *Shofar*. The caller announces the names of the notes—

Tekiyah . . . Shevarim . . . Teruah

The final blast—*Tekiyah Gedolah*—is very, very long. Everyone holds his breath to see how long the sound will last.

Once it happened that a boy from a small village came to the city for the first time.

In the middle of the night he was awakened by the loud beating of drums. He asked the innkeeper what the noise meant. He was told that when a fire breaks out, the people beat their drums, and before long the fire is gone.

When the boy returned home, he told the village leaders about this wonderful system for putting out fires. The people were excited and ordered drums for every household.

The next time a fire broke out, the people beat their drums. As they waited for the fire to go out, many homes burned to the ground. A visitor asked what was happening. When told of the fire and the drums, he exclaimed, "Do you think a fire can be put out by beating drums?

"They only sound an alarm so people will wake up and go to the well for water to put out the fire."

Blowing the Shofar is also an alarm, warning us to change our ways.

TASHLICH

**T**ashlich means to "throw away." The *Tashlich* ceremony is an imaginary way of "throwing away" our sins.

On the afternoon of Rosh Hashanah families gather on the banks of a river, stream, lake, or pond and recite prayers asking forgiveness. Then they shake out the dust from their pockets, or they throw bread-crumbs into the water, as if they were getting rid of their sins.

Rosh Hashanah is only a beginning.

For the next ten days, we think about the year that has passed and the year that is to come. These days are called the Ten Days of Forgiveness.

On the tenth day we celebrate Yom Kippur, the Day of Forgiveness.

TZEDAKAH

In the villages of Eastern Europe it was a custom before the New Year for a messenger to go from house to house with a sack. Those who could afford it put coins into the sack; those who were poor took coins from the sack. No one knew who gave and who took. No one was embarrassed because he was poor. Every family had money to buy the things they needed to celebrate the holiday.

Giving *tzedakah*, sharing what we have with those in need, is an important *mitzvah* in Jewish life.

Before Rosh Hashanah begins, we remember this *mitzvah* by setting aside some of our allowance or savings.

HADLAKAT NEROT
CANDLE-LIGHTING

We welcome Rosh Hashanah with the lighting of the candles.

בָּרוּךְ אַתָּה יְיָ אֱלֹהֵינוּ מֶלֶךְ הָעוֹלָם · אֲשֶׁר קִדְּשָׁנוּ
בְּמִצְוֹתָיו וְצִוָּנוּ לְהַדְלִיק נֵר שֶׁל יוֹם טוֹב

*Baruch atah adonai eloheinu melech
ha'olam asher kid'shanu b'mitzvotav
v'tzivanu l'hadlik ner shel Yom Tov.*

Thank you, God, for bringing our family together to celebrate Rosh Hashanah, and for the *mitzvah* of lighting the candles.
May God bless us with a year of joy.
May God bless us with a year of health.
May God bless us with a year of peace.

KIDDUSH
BLESSING OVER THE WINE

The Kiddush proclaims the holiness of Rosh Hashan-ah. We sing blessings over the cup of wine in honor of the new year.

בָּרוּךְ אַתָּה יְיָ אֱלֹהֵינוּ מֶלֶךְ הָעוֹלָם · בּוֹרֵא פְּרִי הַגָּפֶן

Baruch atah adonai eloheinu melech ha'olam
borei p'ri hagafen.

בָּרוּךְ אַתָּה יְיָ אֱלֹהֵינוּ מֶלֶךְ הָעוֹלָם · שֶׁהֶחֱיָנוּ
וְקִיְּמָנוּ וְהִגִּיעָנוּ לַזְּמַן הַזֶּה:

Baruch atah adonai eloheinu melech
ha'olam shehecheyanu, vekiy'manu,
v'higiyanu laz'man hazeh.

Thank you, God, for the grapes that grow from which wine is made for our new year celebration.

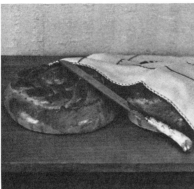

HAMOTZI
BLESSING OVER THE CHALLAH

As we enjoy the Rosh Hashanah *challah* we are grateful for the blessings of life, health, and friendship.

בָּרוּךְ אַתָּה יְיָ אֱלֹהֵינוּ מֶלֶךְ הָעוֹלָם · הַמּוֹצִיא לֶחֶם מִן הָאָרֶץ

*Baruch atah adonai eloheinu melech
ha'olam hamotzi lechem min ha'aretz.*

Thank you, God, for the blessing of bread, and for the festive meal which we will now enjoy together.

BLESSING
FOR A SWEET NEW YEAR

Before we eat our meal, we share apples dipped in honey.

בָּרוּךְ אַתָּה יְיָ אֱלֹהֵינוּ מֶלֶךְ הָעוֹלָם · בּוֹרֵא פְּרִי הָעֵץ

*Baruch atah adonai eloheinu melech
ha'olam borei p'ri ha'etz.*

יְהִי רָצוֹן מִלְפָנֶיךָ יְיָ אֱלֹהֵינוּ וֵאלֹהֵי אֲבוֹתֵינוּ
שֶׁתְּחַדֵּשׁ עָלֵינוּ שָׁנָה טוֹבָה וּמְתוּקָה

*Yehi ratzon milfanecha adonai eloheinu
v'elohei avoteinu shet'chadesh aleinu
shanah tovah um'tukah.*

As we eat this fruit of the trees, we pray that the new year will be a sweet and happy one for all of us.

Many families also dip their challah in honey.

BIRKAT HAMAZON
BLESSING AFTER THE MEAL

We join in giving thanks for the festive meal we have eaten.

בָּרוּךְ אַתָּה יְיָ · הַזָּן אֶת־הַכֹּל :

Baruch atah adonai hazan et hakol.

עֹשֶׂה שָׁלוֹם בִּמְרוֹמָיו הוּא יַעֲשֶׂה שָׁלוֹם
עָלֵינוּ וְעַל־כָּל־יִשְׂרָאֵל · וְאִמְרוּ אָמֵן :

*Oseh shalom bimromav hu ya'aseh shalom
aleinu ve'al kol Yisrael ve'imru amen.*

Thank you, God,
for the festive meal we have shared,
for the food we have eaten at this table,
for the Torah and *mitzvot* which guide our lives,
for Israel, the homeland of the Jewish people,
for our freedom to live as Jews,
for life, strength, and health.
Bless our family, and grant us a good year.

(music pages 28-29)

25

LIGHTING THE CANDLES

Freely adapted after a version by A.W. BINDER

Freely, as a chant

Ba-ruch a-tah a-do nai e-lo-hei-nu me-lech ha-

o-lam, a-sher kid-sha-nu b'mitz-vo-tav v'tzi-va-nu l'-had-lik

ner, l'had-lik ner, shel Yom - tov.

SHEHECHEYANU

Traditional

Ba-ruch a-tah a-do-nai e-lo-hei-nu me-lech ha-o-lam she-

he-che-ya-nu v'-kiy'-ma-nu v'-hi-gi-ya-nu la-z'man ha-zeh.

L'SHANAH TOVAH

Traditional

L'-sha-nah to-vah ti-ka-te - vu, l'-sha-nah to-vah ti-ka-

te - vu, ti-ka-te - vu v'-te-cha-te - mu.

26

KIDDUSH

Traditional

Ba - ruch a - tah a - do - nai e - lo - hei - nu me - lech - ha - o - lam bo -

rei ___ p' - ri ha - ga - fen. A - men. Ba -

ruch a - tah a - do - nai e - lo - hei - nu me - lech ha - o - lam a -

sher ba - char ba - nu mi - kol am ___ v' - ro - m' - ma - nu mi - kol la - shon ___ v' - kid' -

sha - nu b' - mitz - vo - tav. ___ Va - ti - ten la - nu a - do - nai e - lo - hei - nu b'a - ha -

vah ___ mo - a dim l' - sim - cha ___ cha - gim u - z'ma - nim l' - sa - son. ___ Et

yom ha - zi - ka - ron ha - zeh ___ yom te - ru - ah mik - rah ko - desh

ze - cher liy - zi - at mitz - ra - yim. Ki va - nu va - char - tah v - o - ta - nu ki - dash - ta mi -

kol ha - a - mim u - de - var - cha e - met ve - ka - yam ___ l - ad Ba -

ruch a - tah a - do - nai me - lech al kol ha - a - retz m' - ka - desh yis - ra -

el v' - yom ha - zi - ka - ron

BIRKAT HAMAZON

M. NATHANSON

Flowing, in a thankful manner

Ba - ruch a - tah a - do - nai e - lo -
hei - nu me-lech ha - o - lam ha - zan et ha - o - lam ku - lo b'- tu - vo b'-
chen b' - che - sed uv' ra - cha - mim hu no - ten le - chem l' chol ba - sar
ki l' - o - lam chas - do uv' - tu - vo ha - ga - dol ta -
mid lo cha-sar la - nu v' - al yech-sar la - nu ma - zon l' - o - lam va - ed ba - a -
vur sh'-mo ha - ga - dol ki hu el zan um'-far - nes la - kol u - mei -
tiv la - kol u - mei - chin ma - zon l' - chol b'ri - o - tav a - sher ba - ra. Ba -
ruch a - tah a - do - nai ha-zan et ha - kol.

OSEH SHALOM

By N. HIRSH

SHANAH TOVAH

Sha - nah chal - fah sha - nah av -
rah va - a - ni ya - dai a - ri - ma ___
___ sha - nah to - vah le - cha a -
ba sha - nah to - vah lach ___ i -
ma sha - nah to - vah sha - nah to - vah.

TEKIYAH

Te - ki - yah, Te - ki - yah, Te - ki - yah zeh kol sho - far Te -
ki - yah, Te - ki - yah, Te - ki - yah sha - nah to - vah.

TAPUCHIM UD'VASH

Apples and Honey

Folk

1. Ta - pu - chim u - d'vash _____ le - Rosh _____ Ha - sha - nah
2. Ap - ples and hon - ey for Rosh _____ Ha - sha - nah

Ta - pu - chim u - d'vash _____ le - Rosh _____ Ha - sha - nah   Sha -
Ap - ples and hon - ey for Rosh _____ Ha - sha - nah   A

nah   to - vah,   sha - nah   me - tu - kah!
good   new _____ year,   A   sweet   new _____ year!

Ta - pu - chim u - d'vash _____ le - Rosh _____ Ha - sha - nah.
Ap - ples and hon - ey for Rosh _____ Ha - sha - nah.

BEROSH HASHANAH

Traditional

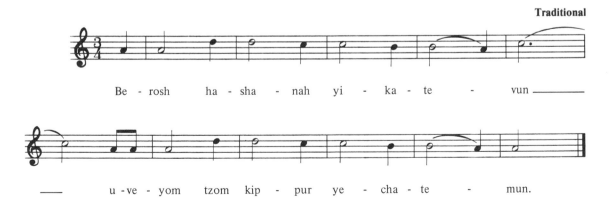

Be - rosh ha - sha - nah yi - ka - te - vun _____

_____ u - ve - yom tzom kip - pur ye - cha - te - mun.